My Pretty Flower Garden

ADULT COLORING BOOK

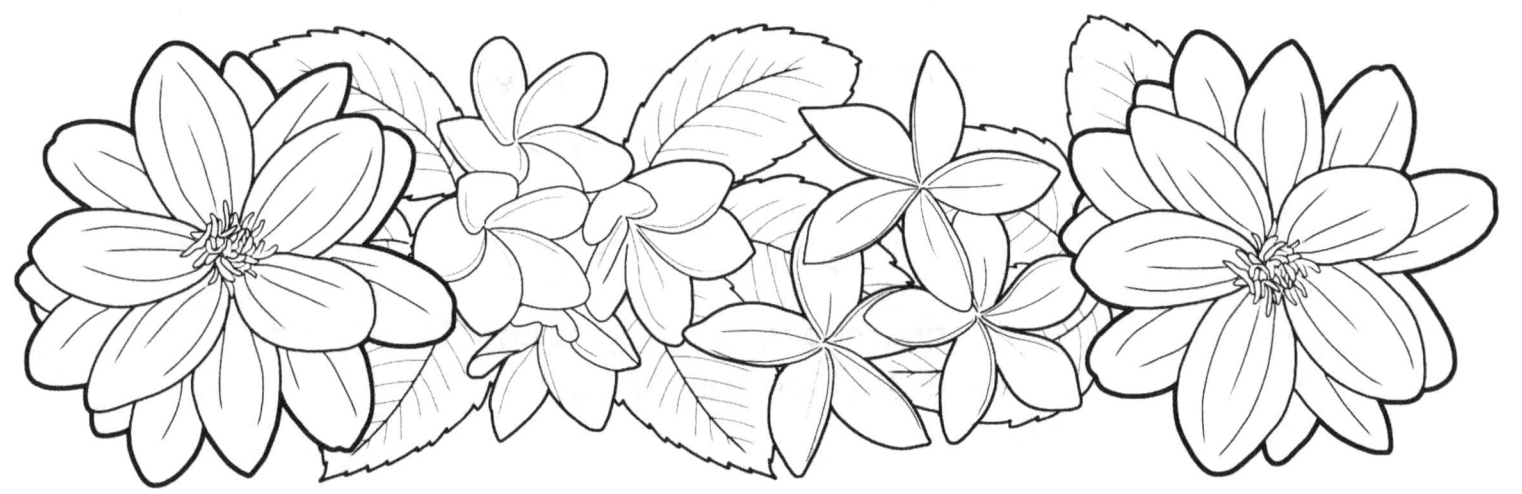

Illustrations by SL Scheibe

First Edition

Published by SL Scheibe

Illustrations by SL Scheibe

www.slscheibe.com | info@slscheibe.com

ISBN-13: 978-0-9950371-2-0
ISBN-10: 0-9950371-2-4

Hello!

SL Scheibe is an artist and illustrator, working away at a cramped desk scattered with paint, markers and a ridiculous number of colored pencils. She spends her days and nights drawing pretty ladies with huge hair and geeky things like vikings, zombies and awkward fairies. She loves drawing comics and creating lineart for coloring artists to color and has many coloring books available on her website.

Happy Coloring!

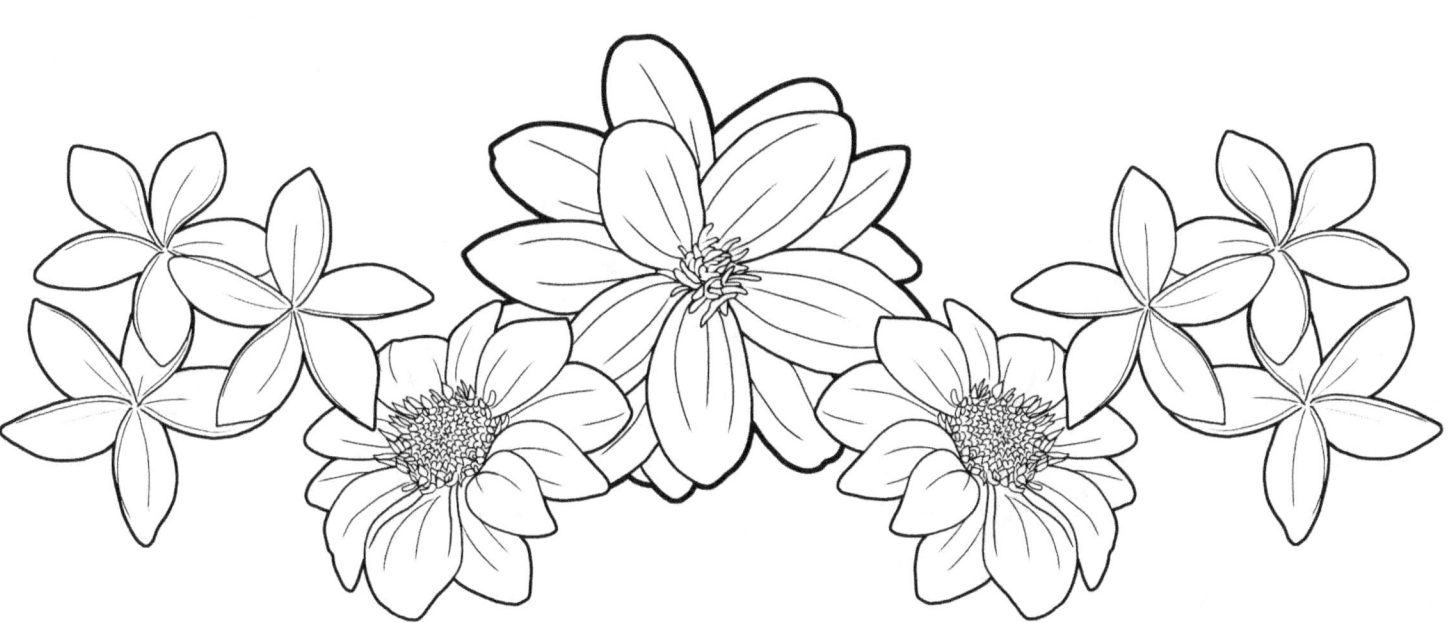

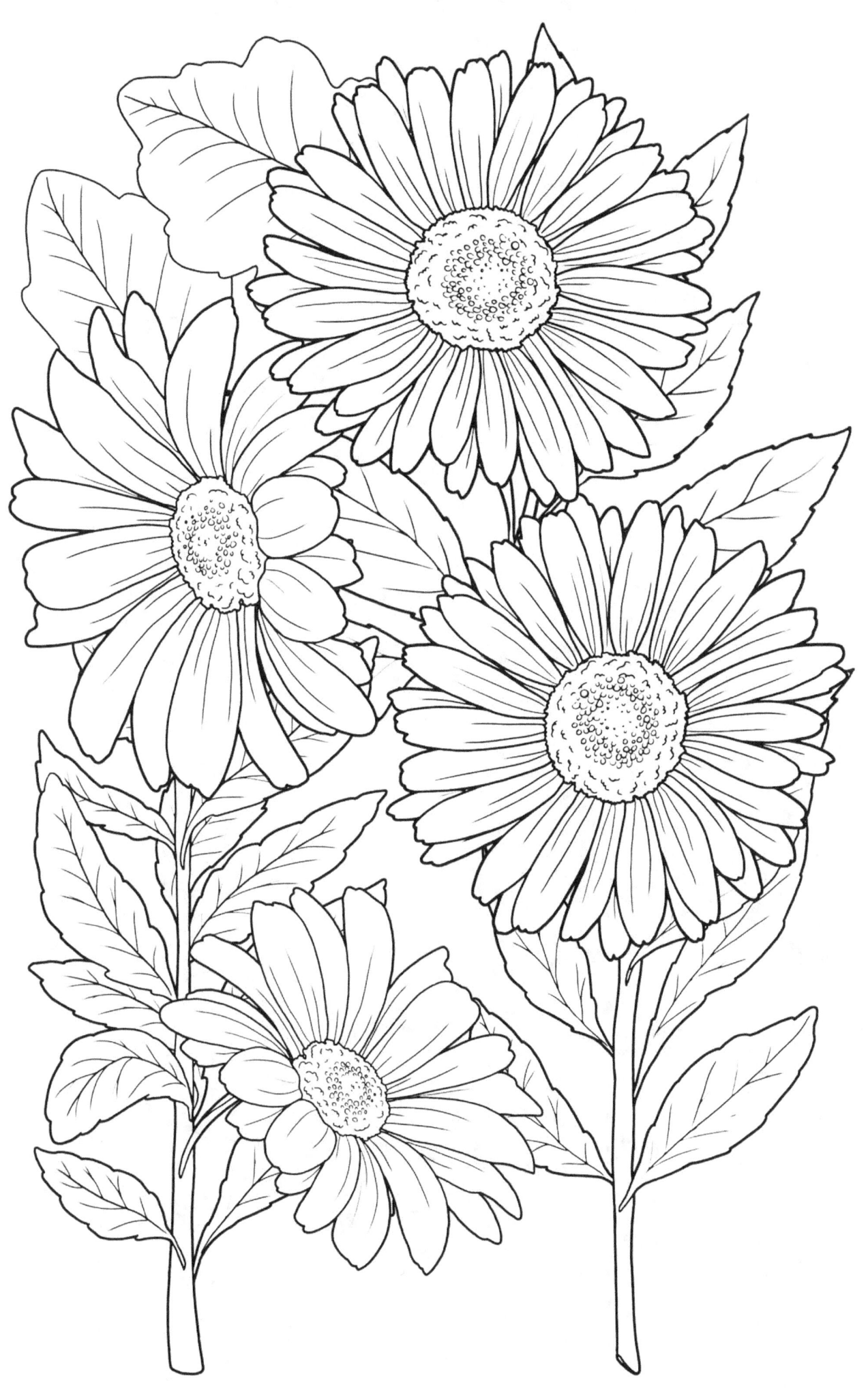

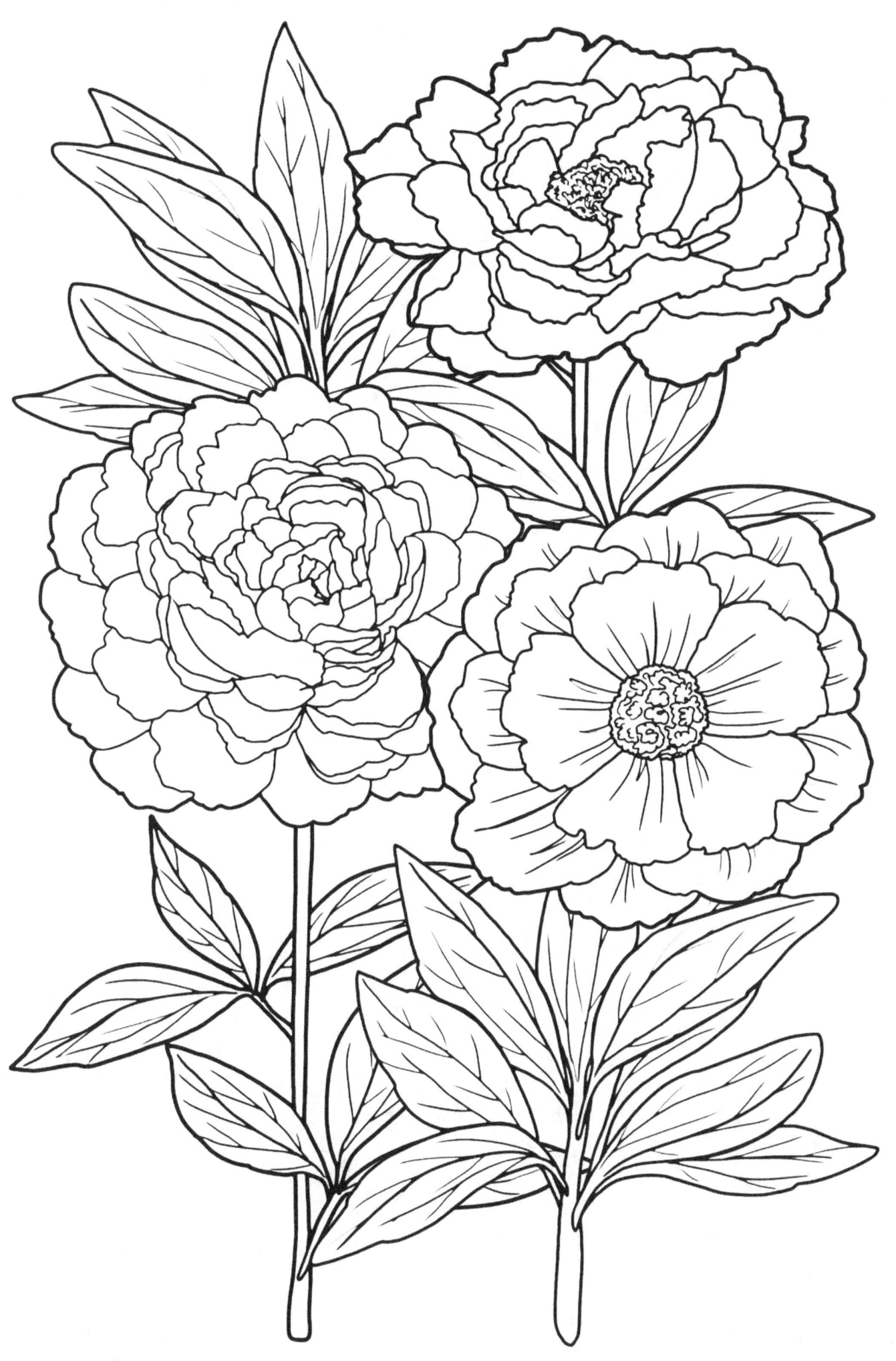

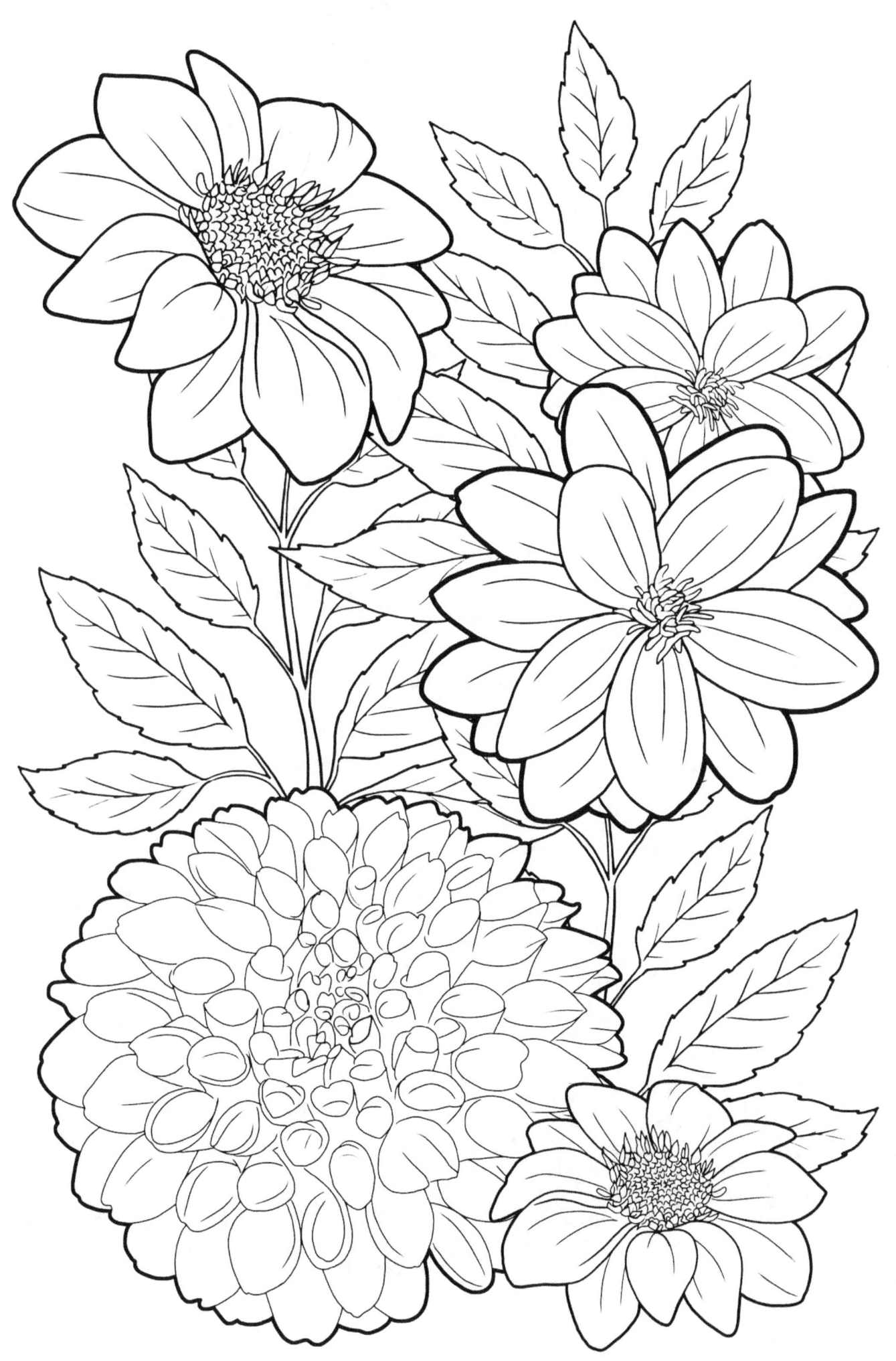

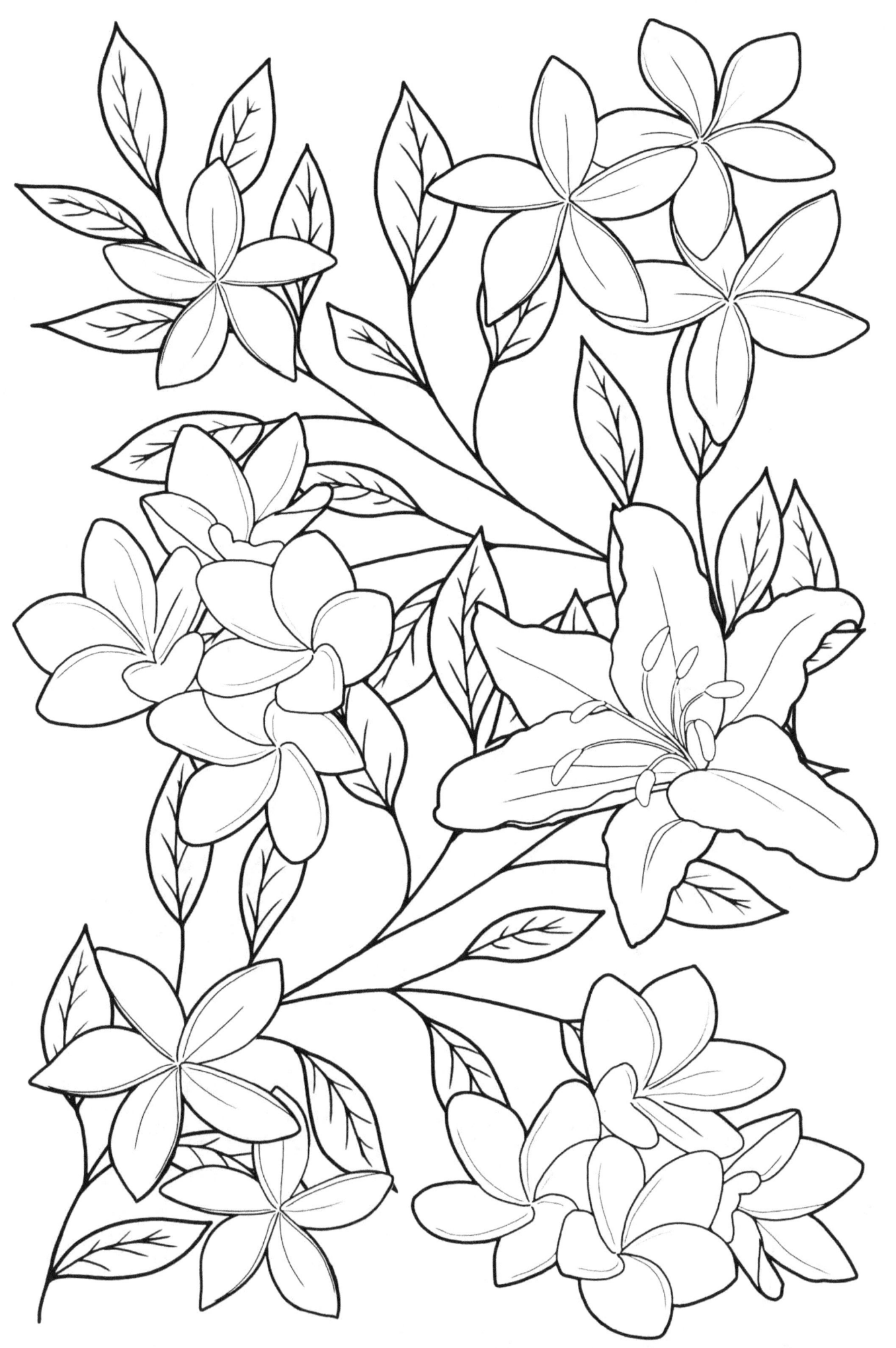

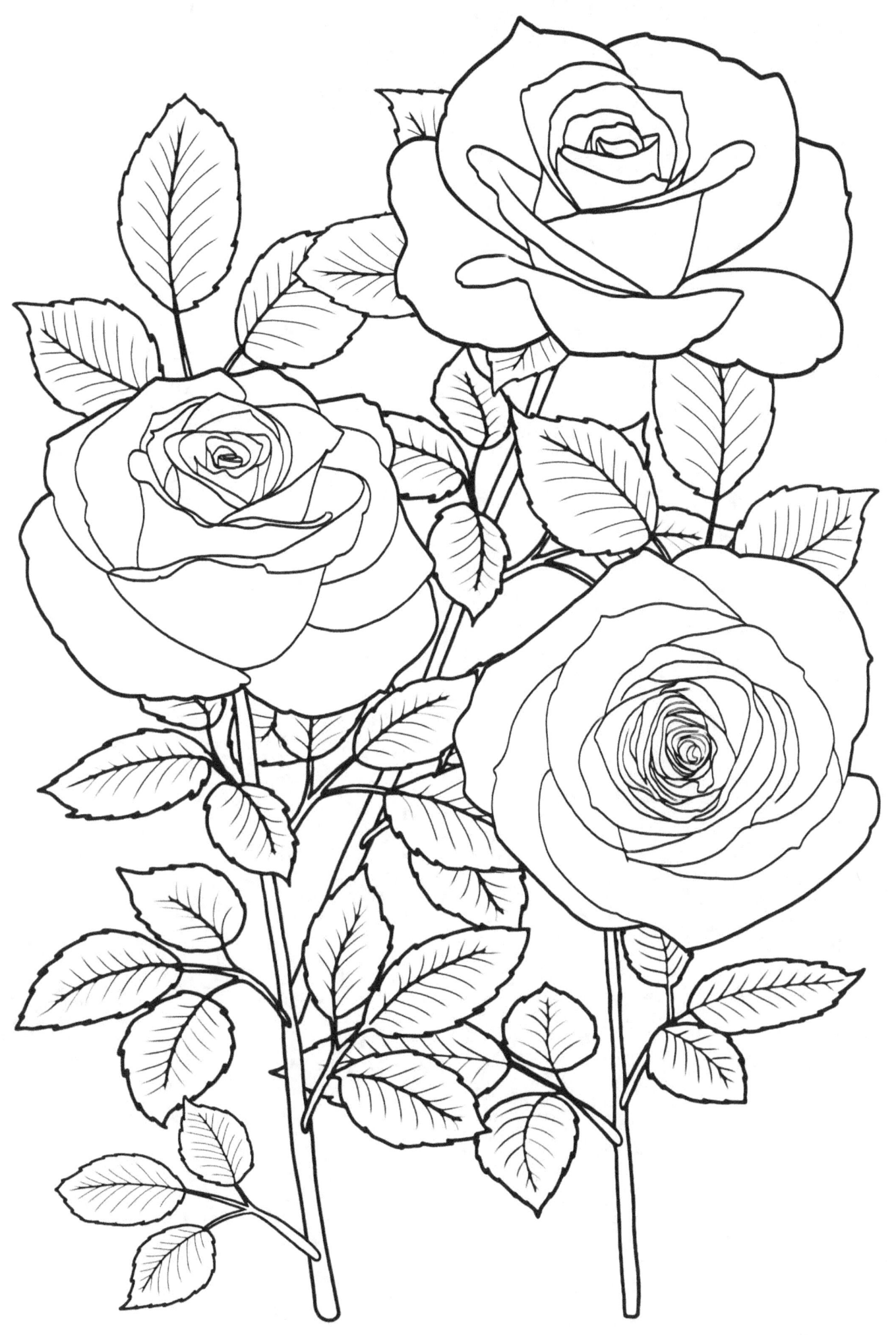

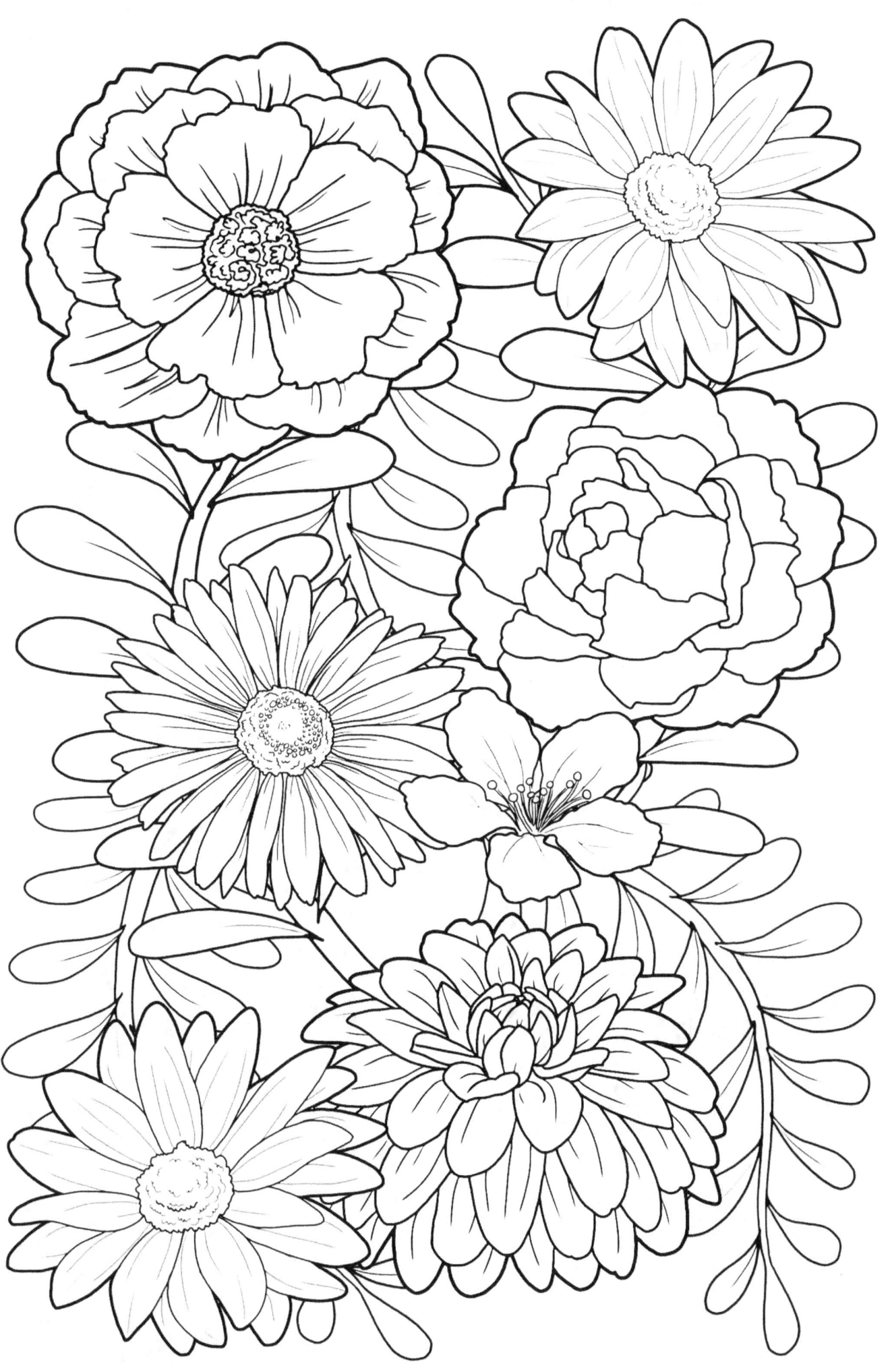

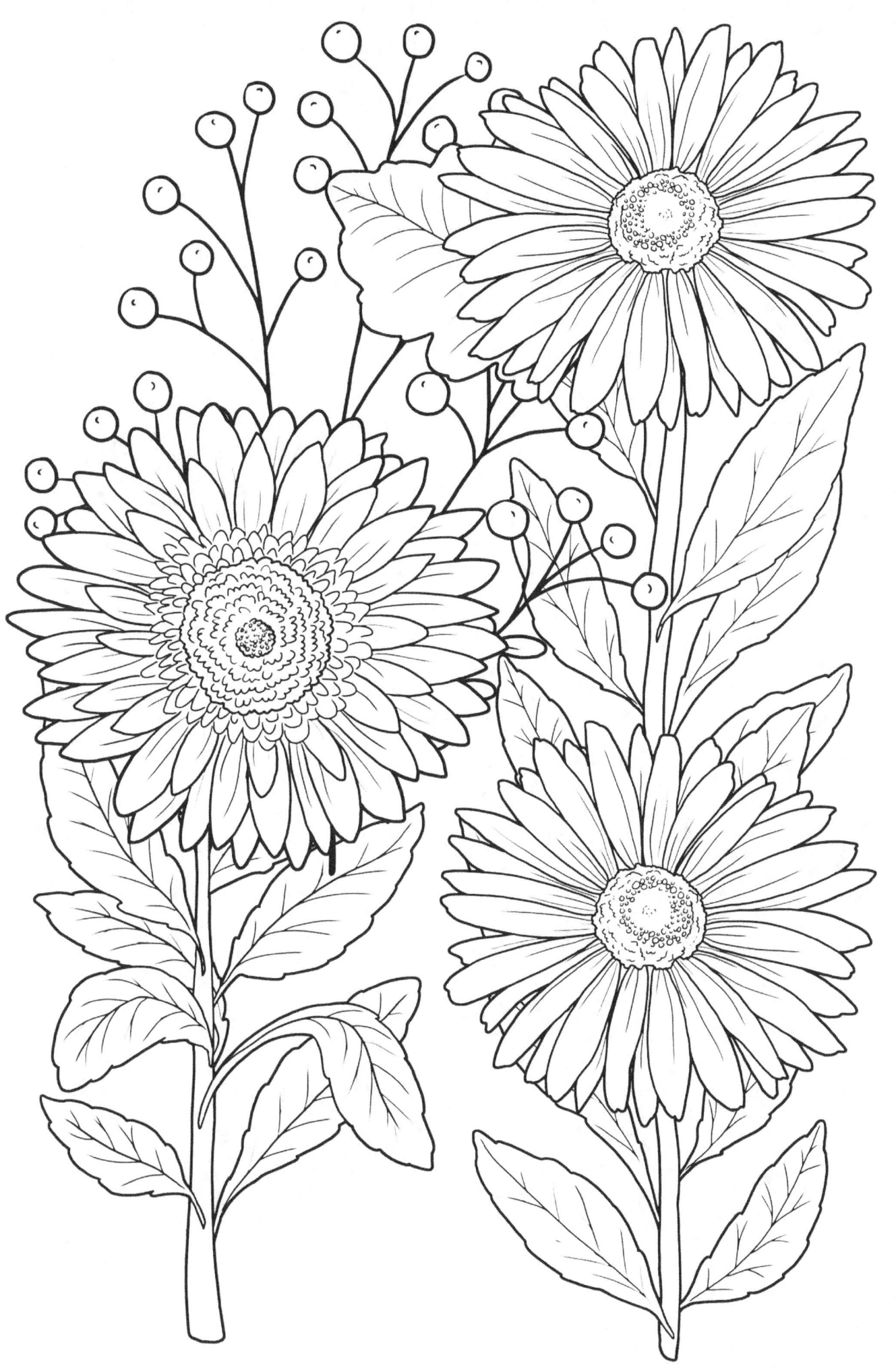

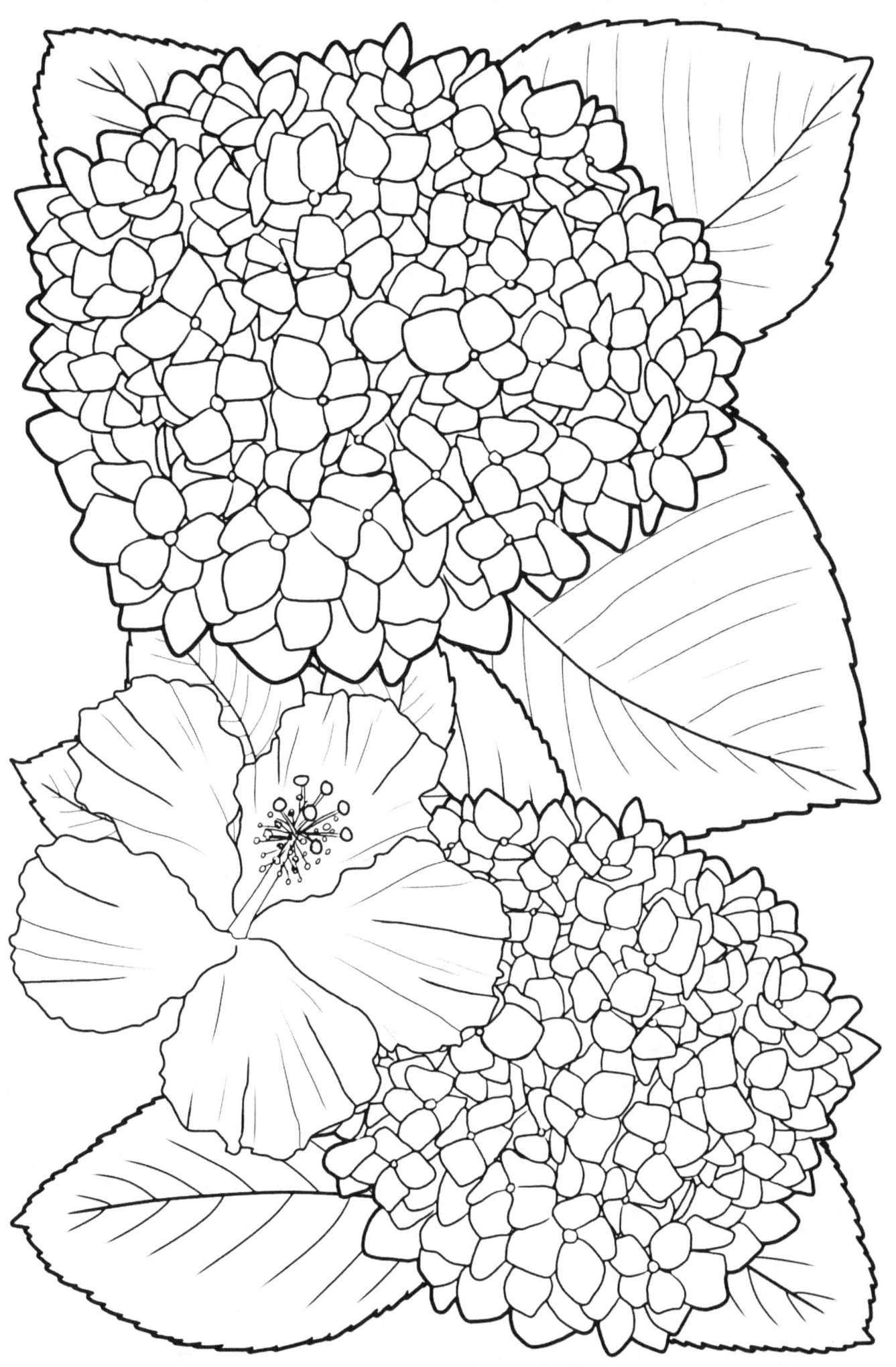

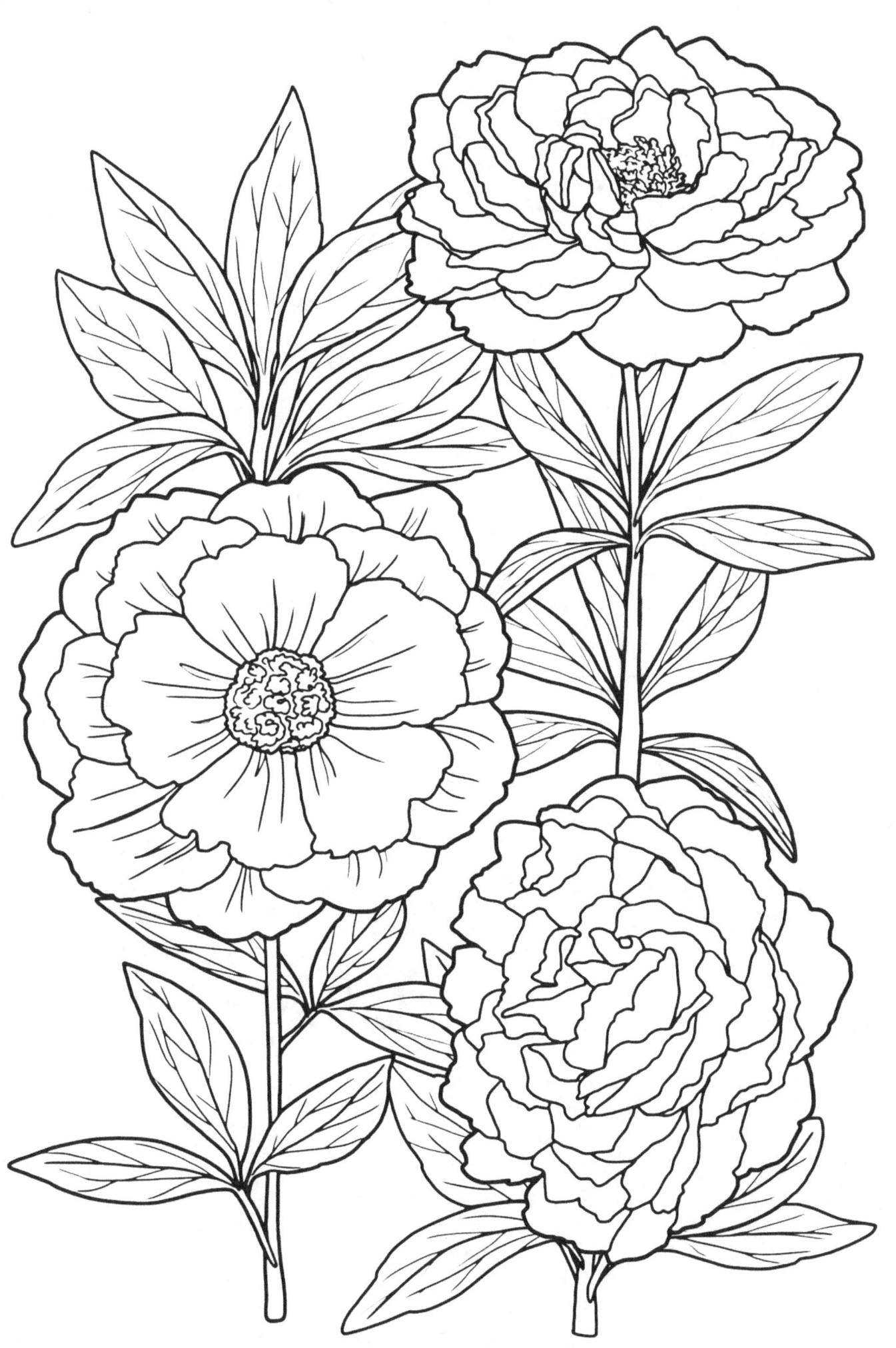

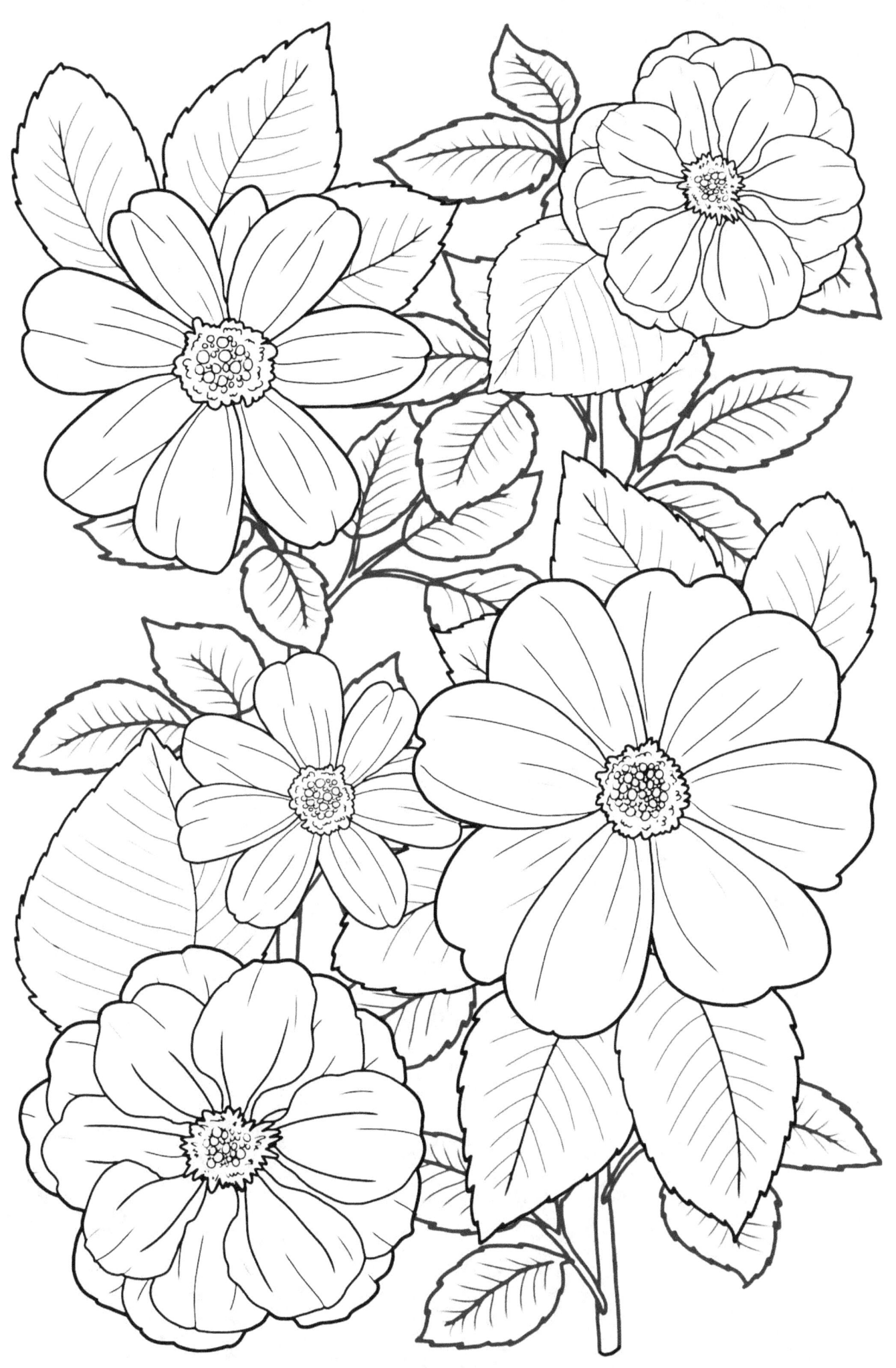

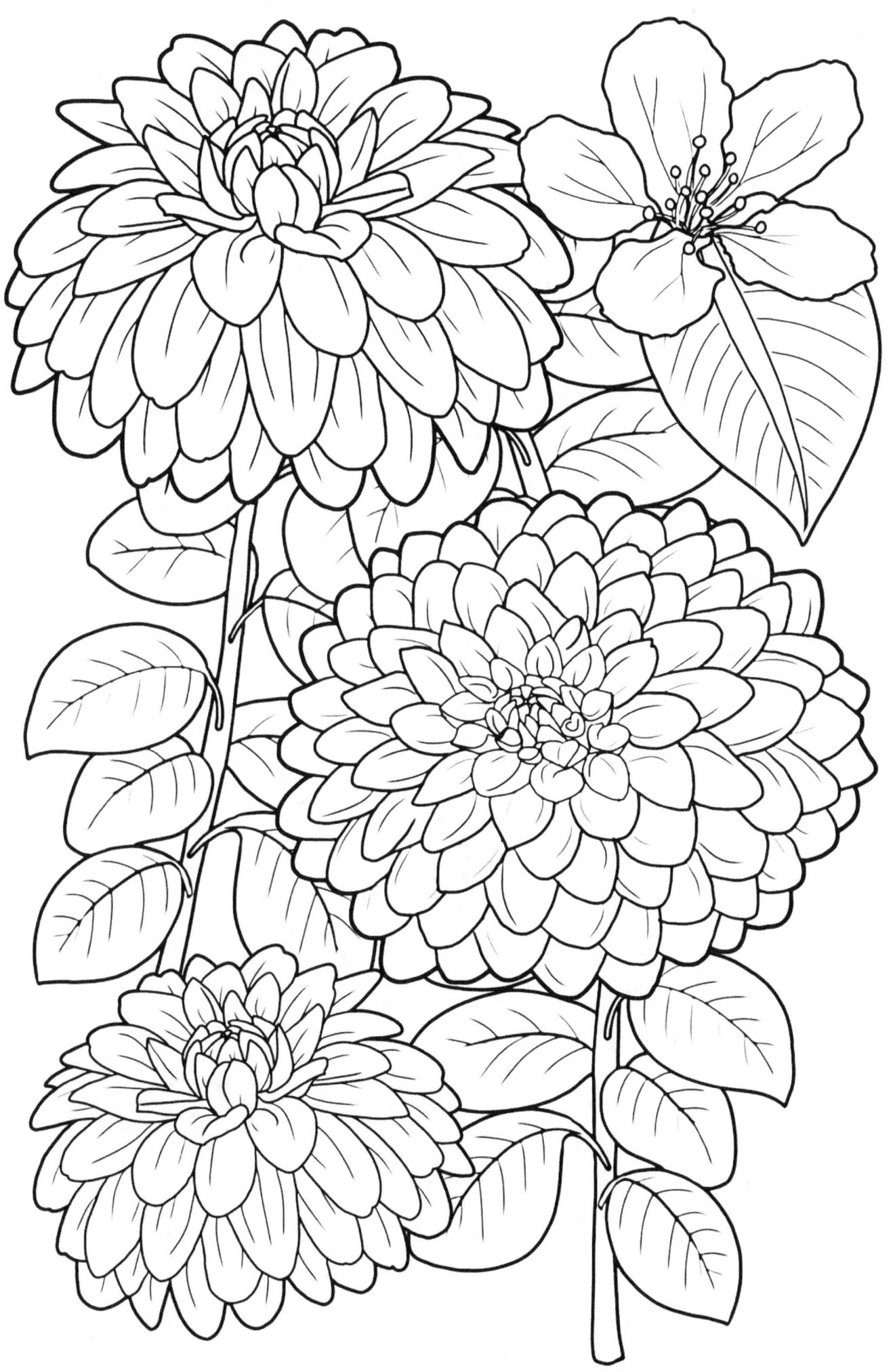

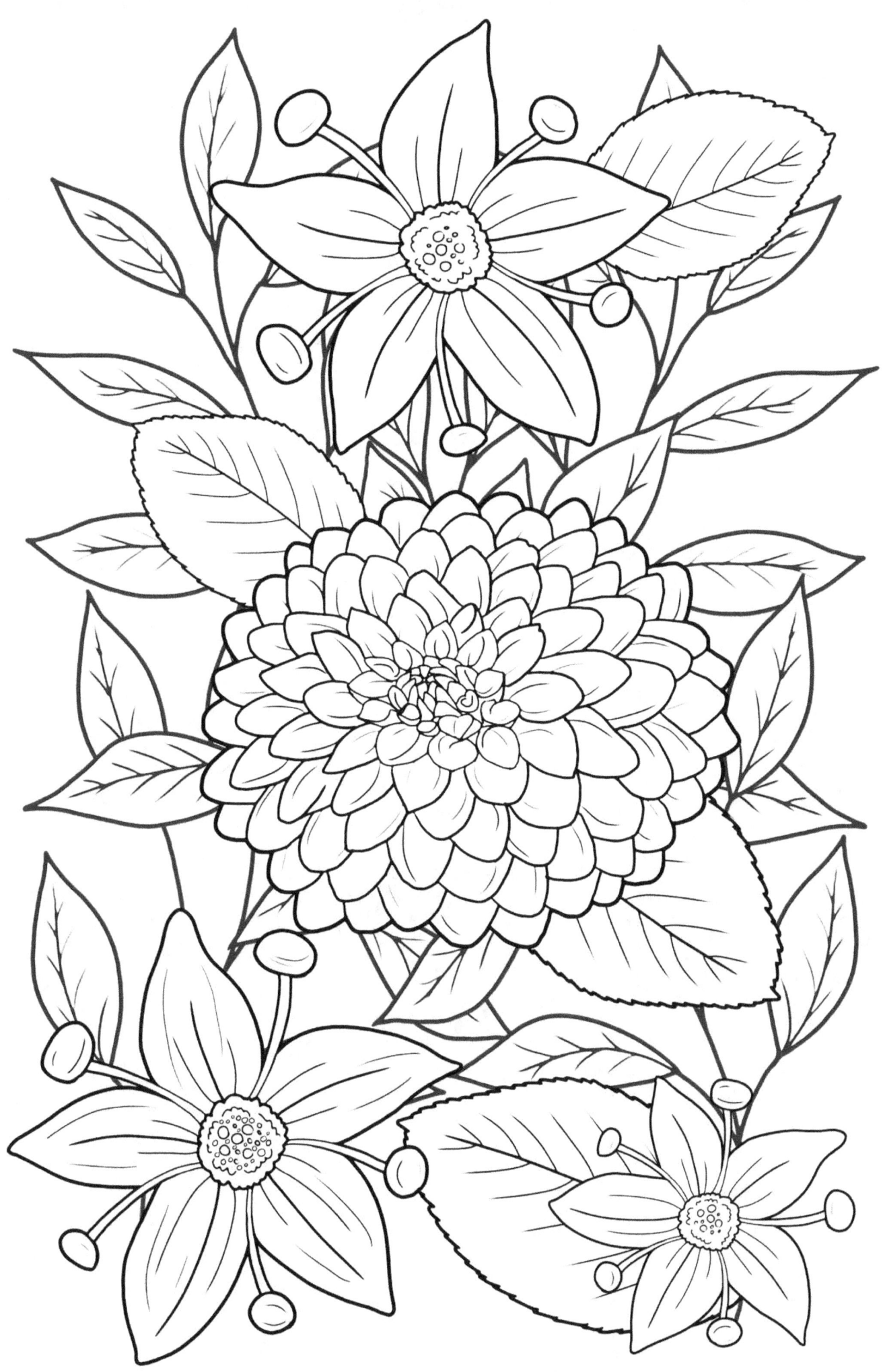

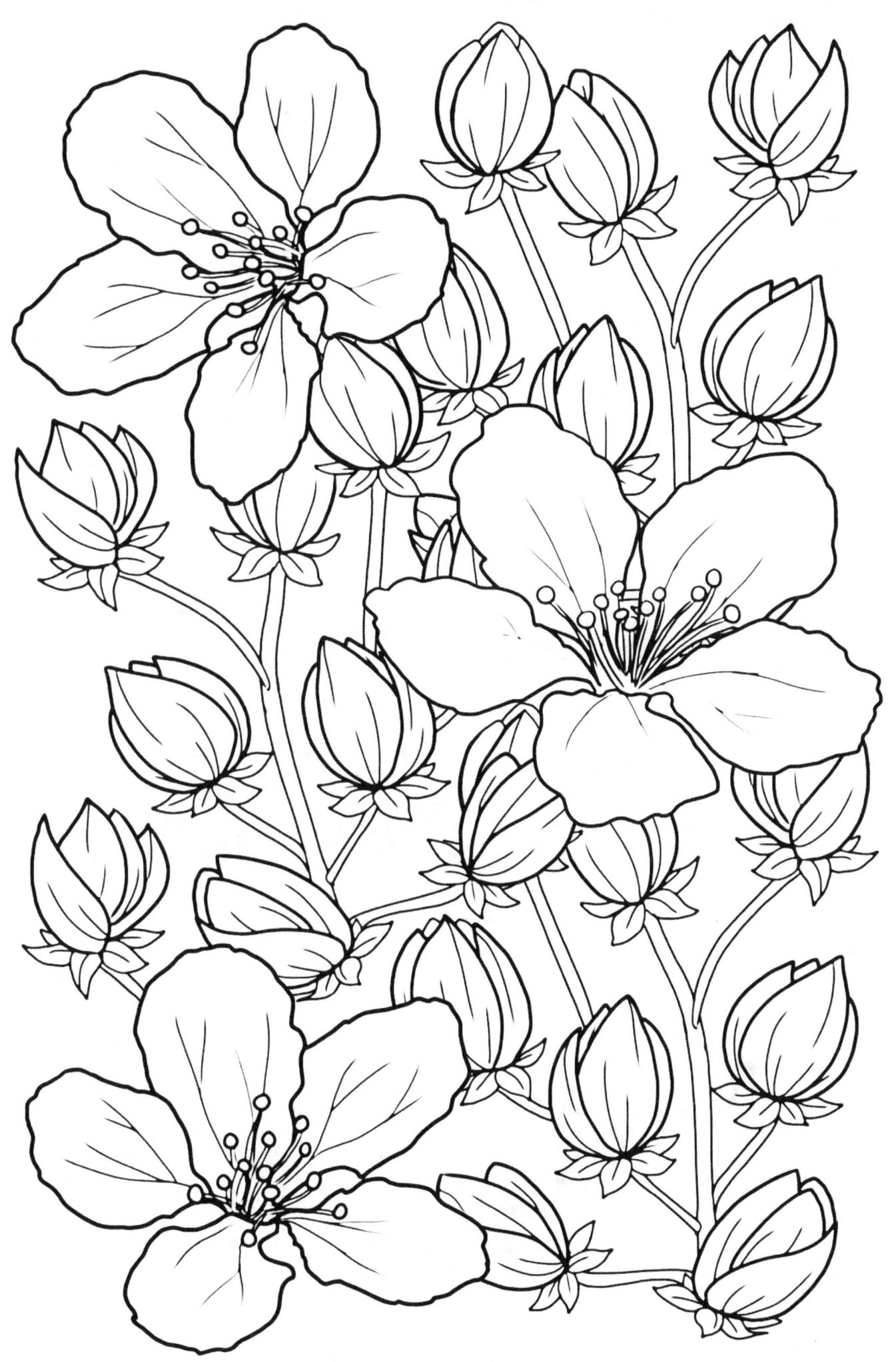

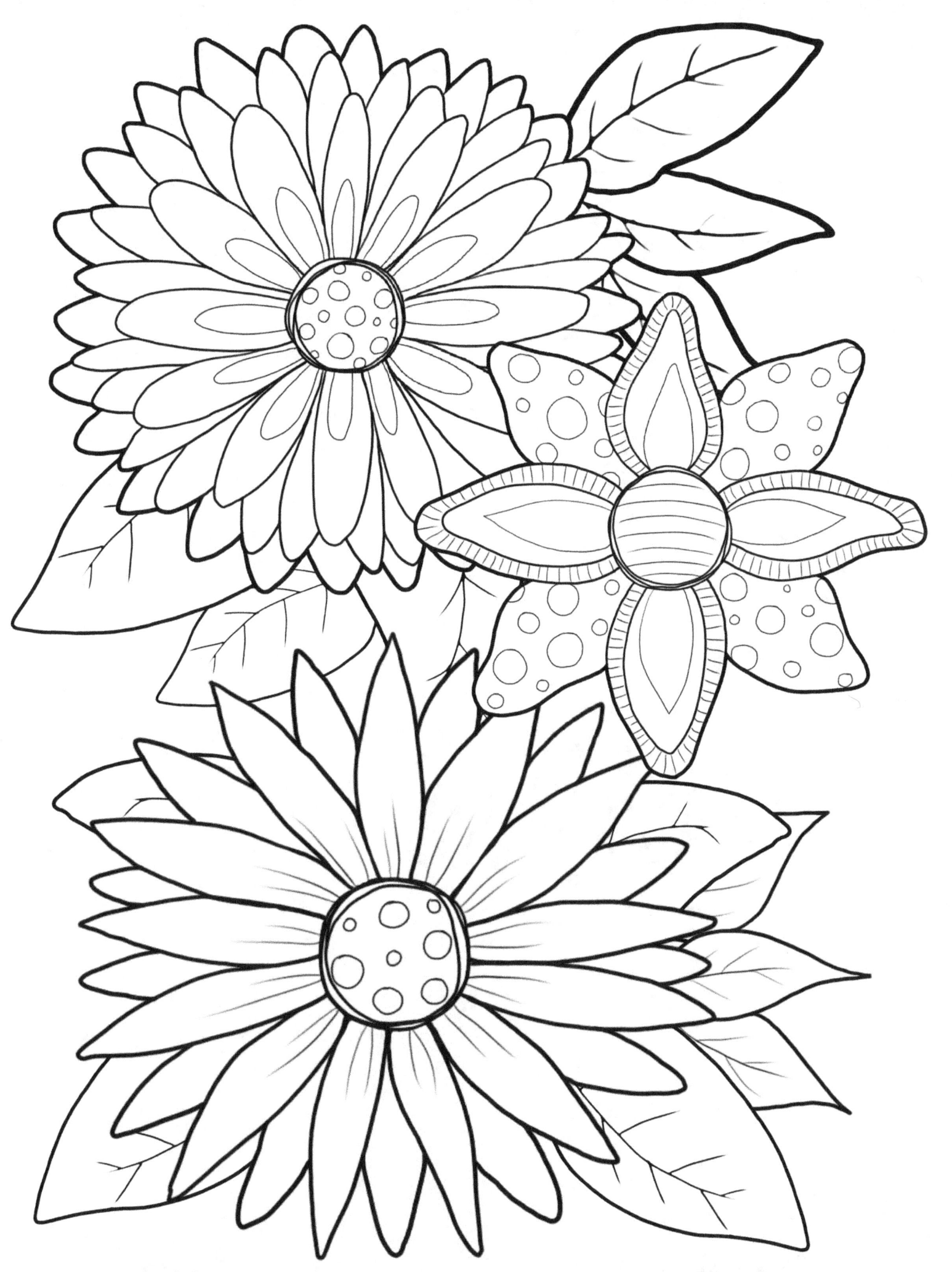

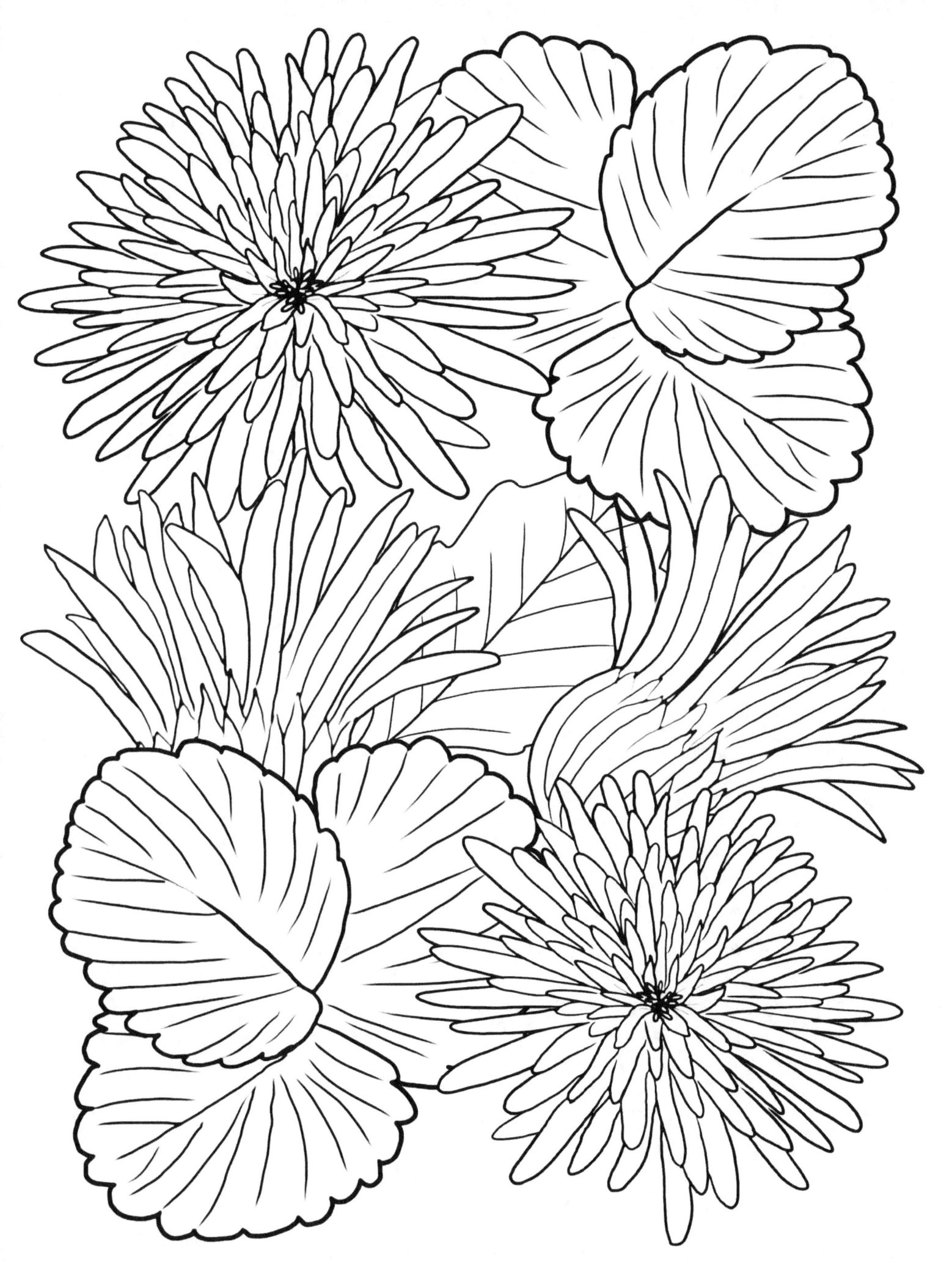

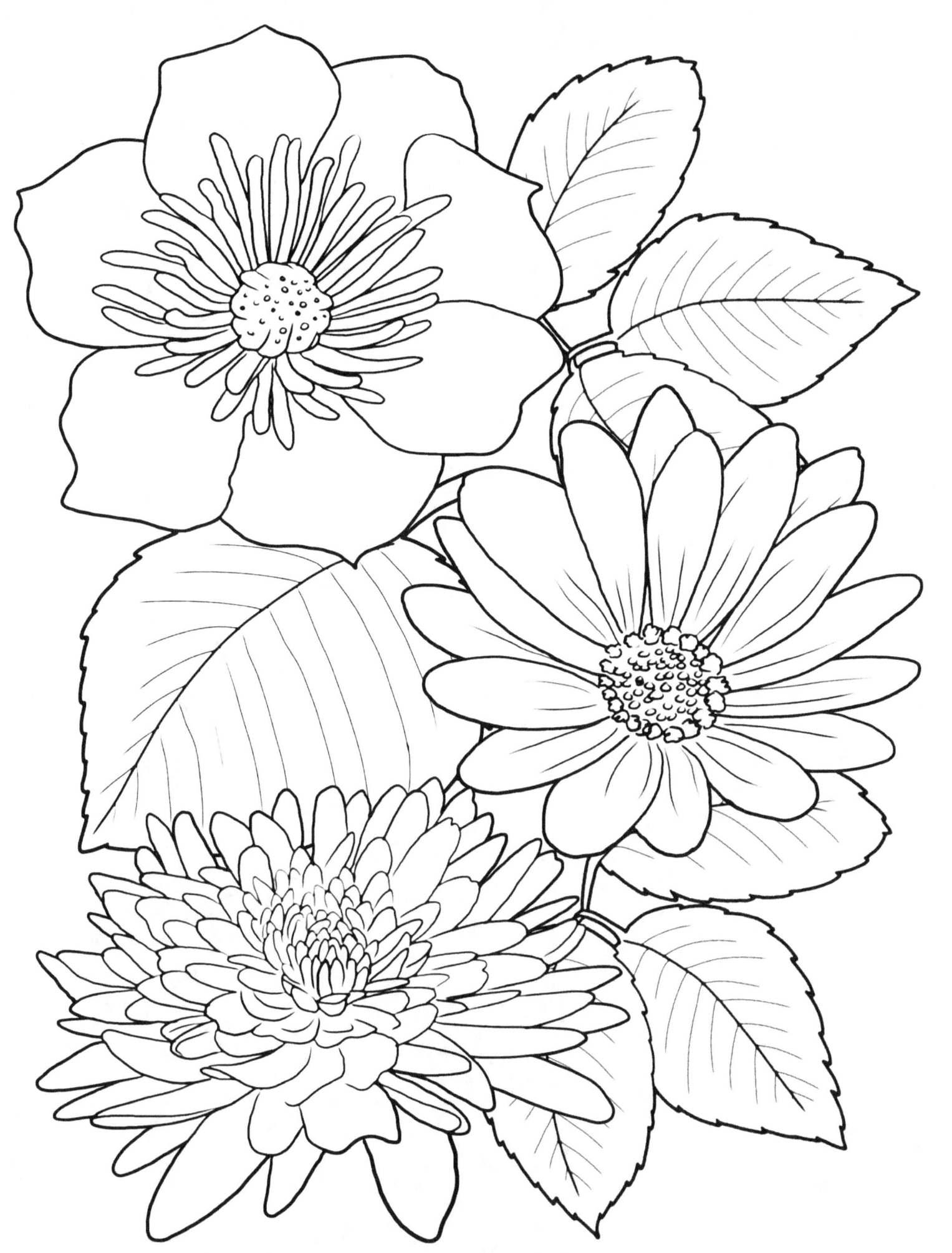

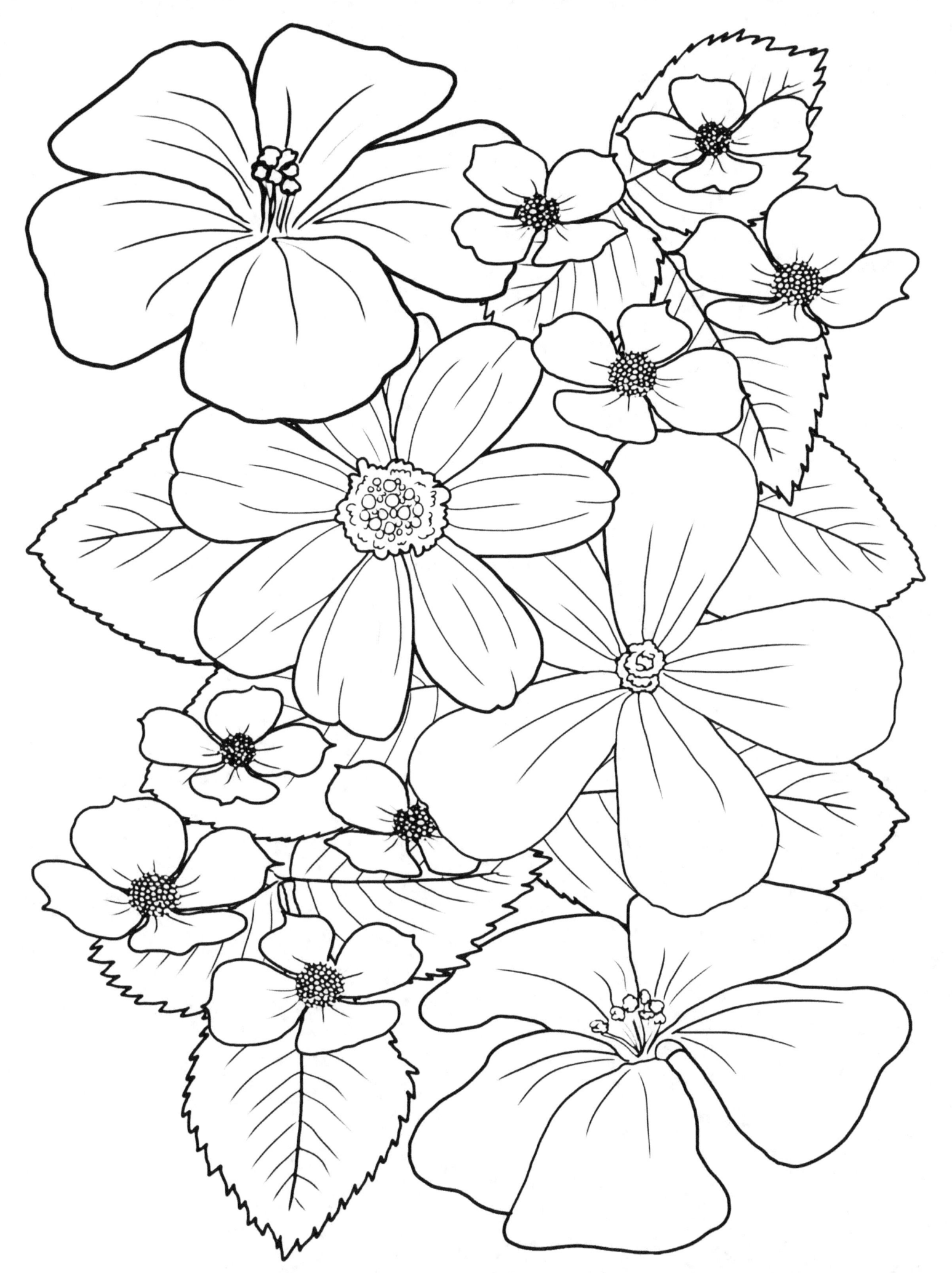

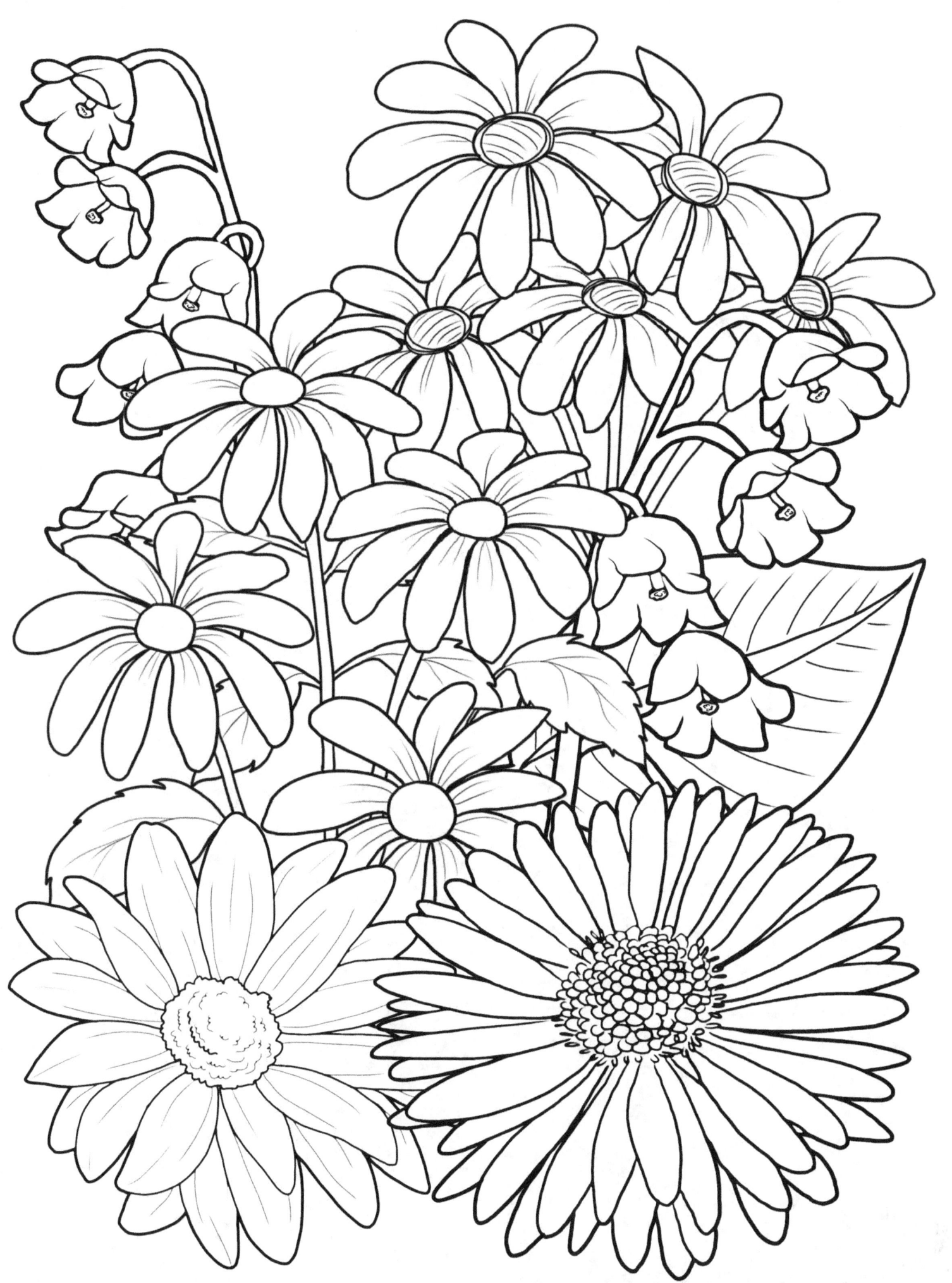

www.ingramcontent.com/pod-product-compliance
Lightning Source LLC
Chambersburg PA
CBHW081146170526
45158CB00009BA/2733